Journ...
Ca...

Devotional readings for advent

Geena Ajay

MAPLE
PUBLISHERS

Journey of a Candle

Author: Geena Chacko (Geena Ajay)

Copyright © Geena Chacko (2022)

The right of Geena Chacko to be identified as author of this work has been asserted by the author in accordance with section 77 and 78 of the Copyright, Designs and Patents Act 1988.

First Published in 2022

ISBN 978-1-915796-10-3 (Paperback)
      978-1-915796-11-0 (E-Book)

Book cover design and Book layout by:
      White Magic Studios
      www.whitemagicstudios.co.uk

Published by:
      Maple Publishers
      Fairbourne Drive, Atterbury,
      Milton Keynes,
      MK10 9RG, UK
      www.maplepublishers.com

A CIP catalogue record for this title is available from the British Library.

Million thanks to

My man, Ajay Cheriyan, for holding my hand every time when I fall, believing in me and my dreams,

Anna and Oliver for your unconditional love,

Mamma (Leelamma Chacko) and Mummy (Prema Cherian) for keeping me in your prayers,

Dr. Zac Varghese, for correcting, mentoring and teaching me throughout the process,

My early readers, Jenso Peter & Ashly Ann Binu for spending your valuable time for giving feedback,

Revd. Eapen Abraham for the all the wishes and prayers,

All my friends, family and relatives who constantly helped me to chase my dream.

People around me always inspired my thoughts and imaginations and every interaction helped me to learn new things. And, some conversations yield simple, but highly valuable thoughts. They will always persist in our memory bag permanently. It's my humble effort to consolidate those moral stories which ignited my mind on paper. Please tap these thoughts to strengthen the people around you. Together we can always be stronger.

GeenA

#staystrong

Message

Greetings to you all in the Precious Name of Lord and Saviour Jesus Christ!

'Journey of a Candle' written by Geena Ajay is a compendium of invaluable meditative illustrations that show us how to serve and navigate ourselves during the various stresses of life. Throughout this devotion, she takes us on a journey of enthralling short stories and incidents based on scripture readings of Biblical figures and addresses them through a candle's lifecycle - from start to finish.

This book will drive anyone from novice to well-insightful to deeply instil the lessons taught and to look at life with a renewed perspective. With intrigue, we will turn every page and be captivated by how exquisite each meditation has been meticulously written and reflected upon. This book is not just a devotional guide; it is a great meditation that will allow us not to be blindsided but be readied for whatever we encounter.

I had the immense privilege of knowing Geena Ajay when I served as the Vicar of St. John's Mar Thoma Church, London, over a decade ago. From that time onward, I praise God for allowing me to mentor and witness such a spiritual development in a person whose heart is set on serving the Lord. As she journeyed faithfully with Christ, it is evident that God has blessed her by giving her insight to pen these beautiful devotions during Advent Lent and in celebrating the Feast of Nativity many years ago. A time when we, as Marthozites, reflect on the coming of the Light into our world, knowing that darkness would never overcome this precious Light because the Holy Son humbled Himself and became one among humans - readied to serve.

After popular demand, it is now being released as a book. I admire and am also inspired by Geena's willingness to share her understanding of God and the scriptures with the community. I earnestly pray that she will continue using her God-given gifts to reach many more by writing more in the future.

I am delighted and blessed to have been allowed to write this short message about her book. I hope and pray that these meditations will assist you all in your journey with Christ, bring you closer to His kingdom, and that you will have an improved Christian perspective on life. I pray that this spiritual tome be as insightful to you all as it was for me.

May God bless us all!
Rev. Eapen Abraham
Vicar
St. Thomas Mar Thoma Church,
Santacruz, Mumbai

Preface

This book, 'Journey of a Candle' is a compendium of daily meditations written by Geena Ajay; it was used during the Advent season at the St. John's Mar Thoma Church, Hounslow, London. She deserves our appreciation and gratitude in finding time to write such a deeply reflective and significant book.

May I make a brief introduction to the author. The author had a difficult childhood, she lost her father at the age of 12. But in spite of her difficulties of her early years, she managed to study well to obtain excellence and also at the same time got involved with children's social movements as the secretary of Manorama's '*Balajanasakhyam*', at the age of 17. She completed her engineering studies and became proficient as a Software Engineer. She came to the UK in 2008, took further qualification and got promoted with distinction in each and every job she took; now she is working in Belfast (N. Ireland) as a senior Software Engineer for Global Payments. She is also a home-maker, a wife and mother of two beautiful children, and she has a very active involvement with the church. She has been one of the editors of the 'ECHO', the official journal of the Mar Thoma Church in the UK and Europe, from its inception in 2013. As a committed Christian, she always likes to act as a gap-filler in a community and to support people when they are in need without coming to spotlight.

The title itself is a clue to the importance of the book. The foundation of the Christian faith is encapsulated in the Advent story. The Advent season focuses on expectation and the thought that it serves as an anticipation of Christ's birth in the season leading up to Christmas. The word "Advent" is derived from the Latin word *adventus*, meaning "coming," which is a translation of the Greek word *Parousia* meaning presence or arrival of a king. Advent prepares us for the coming God into the world as the 'babe of Bethlehem' to share our human condition and help us to redeem ourselves. Our entire lives are transformed because of the events of Advent, in God becoming one of us, the Immanuel. 'The Word becoming flesh and making his dwelling among us' is the central event in the history of mankind (cf. Jn1:1-14).

Each Advent season is an opportunity for us to recollect and relive the experiences. This book is certainly a help in that direction. Entering in to the spirit of the Advent season is accepting an invitation from God to become vigilant and attentive of every event which reminds us that the God of love is being born into all aspects our daily living. Advent is not a holiday season for having a good time with family and friends, singing carols and or giving presents and all such things. Advent is a gift from God to find time to rediscover the real meaning of all the events associated with the life and ministry of Jesus Christ to create a community of 'at-one-ment'. It is a time to declare with the faith community that God has come, God is Here and God will come again. Advent wreath and candles are symbolic representation of events to remind us that God who is the creator, Sustianer, protector and lover who came down to heal this fractured world.

Advent is a season of waiting, and hoping for the best, also a quiet stretch of spiritual preparation leading to Christmas. The story of Christmas is known to every one of us. It is one of the busiest times. It's during this season that most of us wrap gifts, bake cakes, make travel plans to be with family and friends and do million and one things leading to the celebration on Christmas Day. Mary's reply to the angel reminds us to trust in God's love.

And to surrender control to Him by saying, "Let it be done to me according to Thy word." Mary had some fears, but she trusted in God's will. Her fears were melted and purified because she trusted in God.

The author begins these mediations with the statement: "Advent is a season of waiting, and hoping for the best, also a quiet stretch of spiritual preparation leading to Christmas." She is submitting herself and identifying with Mary, the mother of Jesus, in these words: *"Let it be done to me according to Thy word" (Lk 1:38).* The author believes that story telling is an ideal way to share the lived-out experiences in the real world. Therefore, one of the unique features of these daily mediations is that the author's skilful ability to search out and link appropriate stories from the 'social-space' to go with the mediations based on biblical texts. This a hermeneutic way of studying the biblical text and the texts become alive for us to reach out and touch.

Each day of the Advent meditation is based on a biblical verse relating to the Adent story in the first two chapters of the gospels of Matthew and Luke. It is further supplemented with other verses: Gal 5:22-23, Eph 4:2, Mk10:18, Ps 86:11, Phil 4:4-5, Titus 2:11-13, Mt 5:48, and Lk 7:19.

The overall emphasis of these meditations is the proclamation that 'God changed us from frozen wax to an amazing fragrance filled candle of Hope. Let's step together to Bethlehem with the candles of peace, faith, love, joy and hope. The advent wreath and candles, place all of us in the right place ready to be lighted . . . we are lighted to lighten by the light of life.' She ends this meditation with the statement: "Each of us has a purpose for being on this planet, when we know that purpose, we have the opportunity to manifest it. We should pass His Love, Joy, Peace, and Hope to others. Oh Lord, thank You for Your great Mercy on us, help us to carry Your light and light others. Amen."

I express my deep gratitude to Geena Ajay for this very helpful spiritual guide for encouraging others to become a 'candle' to establish God's kingdom values on the earth. Let us get lighted with the ever-shining light of Jesus to lighten others. I very much enjoyed studying these mediations and the stories attached to them. I have no hesitation in recommending this for private and group studies during the Advent season. Let me conclude this with a poem from William Brodrick:

"We have to be candles,
burning between
hope and despair,
faith and doubt,
life and death,
all the opposites.
That is the disquieting place
where people must always find us."

Professor (Dr.) Zac Varghese,
20-07-22

Day 1
Melt the frozen wax . . . melt the frozen heart

"Let it be done to me according to Thy word." Luke 1:38

Mary – melting her fears and accepting God

Advent is a season of waiting, and hoping for the best, also a quiet stretch of spiritual preparation leading to Christmas. The story of Christmas is known to every one of us. It is one of the busiest times. It's during this season that most of us wrap gifts, bake cakes and a million and one things leading to the celebration on Christmas Day. Mary's reply to the angel reminds us to trust in God's love. And to surrender control to Him by saying, *"Let it be done to me according to Thy word."* Mary had some fears, but she trusted in God's will. Her fears were melted and purified because she trusted in God.

We can imagine a mother-to-be preparing a room for her baby by gathering a crib, clothing and toys for the little one who will one day fill her life. First, though, she must empty the room of anything that she doesn't need. Mary is one of the greatest symbols during Advent because she had to empty herself of worries and fears to prepare her heart to become God's mother. To do this, she uttered the prayer of perfect hope and trust: *"Let it be done to me according to Thy word."*

During Advent, we must also empty our hearts of whatever is useless and worn out. Yes, time to melt our fears and worries.

We are wax, filled with guilt, fears, worries and much more stuff. Let us melt ourselves and purify for the day. Maybe a sense of guilt, maybe a sense of fear of society, or it might be a worry about kids, jobs broken relationships and finances. But we should not forget there is a beloved God who is ready to help us to melt these uncertainties in our life and he knows us more than anyone. That's why Prophet Jeremiah said, *"Before I formed you in the womb, I knew you, before you were born, I set you apart" (Jer 1:5).*

Leaving to God's hands

A man who was a warrior just got married and was returning home with his wife. They were crossing a lake in a boat and suddenly a great storm arose. His wife became very much afraid because it seemed almost hopeless. The boat was small and the storm was huge, and at any moment they were going to be drowned. But the man sat silently, calm and quiet as if nothing was happening. The woman was trembling and she said, "Are you not afraid? This may be our last moment of life! It doesn't seem that we will be able to reach the other shore. Only some miracles can save us; otherwise, death is certain. Are you not afraid? Are you mad or what? Are you a stone or something?" The woman was even more puzzled. What he was doing! Then he brought a sword close to the woman's neck, so close that just a small gap was there, it was almost touching her neck. He said, "Are you afraid?" She started to laugh and said," Why should I be afraid? The sword is in your hands, why should I be afraid? I know you love me." He put the sword back and said, that is my answer **I know God Loves us, and the storm is in His hands, so whatever is going to happen is going to be for good. If we** *survive, it is good; if we don't survive, good, because everything is in His hands and He won't do anything wrong. . .*

We often say "Amen" with strings attached in our part, but Mary did differently. Today we can sing the lines of Daniel Iverson's famous Hymn together. *"Spirit of the living God, fall afresh on me. Melt me, mould me, fill me, use me."* In our family prayer repeat the prayer of Mary, in a real way, give Him the permission to come in, melt imperceptibly from within us, and orients us toward our true and eternal good. Let us pray towards that goal with our God.

Day 2
Melt the frozen wax . . . melt the frozen heart

"When Joseph woke up, he did what the angel of the Lord had commanded him and took Mary home as his wife"
(Matthew 1:24).

Joseph melted his doubts with the words of God

Yesterday we saw how Mary prepared for the advent by melting her fears. We too melted our fears and purified with the melted wax. We need to get melted and purified during this advent season for turning into the right candle at Bethlehem.

Today Joseph is reminding us a saying: "Life is what happens while we're busy making other plans." Joseph was making plans for his future, but suddenly his world turned upside down. Mary's pregnancy filled him with questions. There was a conflict raging in Joseph's soul. Then when he thought of divorcing her quietly, he realized God's intervention and God told him to take Mary as his divinely blessed wife. Here Joseph resigned himself to the will of God. When he accepted God's words, he got the greatest designation in the world – earthly, adopted, father of Jesus. He is a model of obedience to God's word. He is a reminder that the spirit of loving attention is not just for Advent, or even for Christmas, but it is something to inculcate till our last breath.

God's plan

Once there were three trees on a hill in the woods. The first one wanted to be a treasure chest. The second one wanted to be a mighty ship. The third one wanted to be the tallest and wanted to be remembered by everyone. After many years three woodsmen came and cut the trees. The first tree was made into a feed box for animals. He was then placed in a barn and filled with hay. The second tree was cut and made into a small fishing boat. The third tree was cut into large pieces and left alone in the dark. Then years went by, and the trees forgot about their dreams. Then one day, a man and a woman came to the barn. She gave birth and they placed the baby in the hay in the feed box that was made from the first tree. The man wished that he could have made a crib for the baby, but this manger would have to do. The tree could feel the importance of this event and knew that it held the greatest treasure of all time. Years later, a group of fishermen with their captain got into the fishing boat made from the second tree. The captain was tired and went to sleep. While they were out on the water, a great storm arose and the boat didn't think it was strong enough to keep the men safe. The men woke the sleeping captain, and he stood up and said: "Peace" and the storm stopped. At this time, the tree knew that it had carried the King of Kings in its boat. Finally, someone came and got the third tree, made into a cross. It was carried through the streets as the people mocked the man who was carrying it. When they came to a stop, the man who was carrying the cross was nailed to it and raised in the air to die at the top of a hill. When Sunday came, the tree, out which the cross was made, came to realize that it was strong enough to stand at the top of the hill and be as close to God as possible, because Jesus had been crucified on it.

If you place your trust in our loving God, He will give you great gifts. Each of the trees got what they wanted, but not in the way they had imagined. We don't always know what God's plans are for us. We just know that His ways are not our ways, but His ways are always the best. All we need to do is to say "yes" to God. Joseph was willing to let his life be disrupted – to make that 'Yes', a reality – to live not according to his own will, but God's.

May this advent melt our frozen hearts filled with doubts and questions and may it purify our hearts to seek the will of God, help us to do the will of God, join the will of God, no matter what everyone else is doing, no matter how much we are commanded to do otherwise by our society or friends. During this Christmas we just need to follow the plan of our God, everything else is assured.

Day 3
Melt the frozen wax . . . melt the frozen heart

"And Zechariah said to the angel, "How shall I know this? For I am an old man, and my wife is advanced in years." (Luke 1:18).

Zechariah – the priest who froze with unbelief

We started these series of meditations with Mary, the mother of Jesus; she asked "How can this be?" Whereas today Zechariah asks, "How shall I know this?" Mary believes the promise; she just wonders how it will happen. We would expect the seasoned-priest standing in the Holy of Holiest to boldly stand on the promise delivered by Gabriel and joyfully take on the responsibility of raising this special son, John the Baptist. And we would expect the young girl who had just learned that she would become pregnant before marriage in an unforgiving culture to panic in distress. But the priest panicked and the girl stood firm.

Zechariah knew the Scriptures. He knew that Sarah, Rebekah, Rachel, Hannah, and others had children in old age after years of barrenness. He knew that God had worked many other miracles. He regularly taught the Bible to the people, prayed for the people, set an example for the people in how he lived and loved God and he conducted services at the temple. But this righteous believer raised his doubts. He was not expecting God to answer his prayers, because secret unbelief and doubts lay hidden away in his heart. After all, his heart was frozen with unbelief.

God put a melting plan for Zachariah. Zachariah did not speak a word for nine months! What if God did the same thing to us in our unbelief? How long would we remain silent? Zachariah could not bless the people who waited anxiously outside for the blessing. He could not speak a word. He could give no instruction, or a word of praise, or even tell them what God has said to him.

God's Signal

Once upon a time, following a shipwreck, one of the crew was washed ashore on a desolate island. He stayed there for many months expecting a rescue by some other ship. He built a tent and started a new way of life. Most of the time he was at the beach and looked for signs of help from any approaching ship. He prayed fervently but his prayers were not answered for a long period. One day, he found that his tent was on fire. He rushed to the scene but was helpless. He cursed God and his fate, as his last possessions were lost in the fire. He returned to the beach, ready to commit suicide in the ocean. As he entered the water, he could see the flag of a distant ship. A boat was fast approaching him. The sailors arrived and rescued him. Back on the ship, he asked the captain how they could learn about his plight. The captain said, "We saw some fire and smoke rising from that island. We sent the boat expecting someone there." It was only then that he realized that God's ways are mysterious. He felt sorry for cursing God for letting his only possessions catch fire. He realized that the fire was God's signal to the sailors on a distant ship. He learned to trust His lasting love. "I alone know the plans I have for you, plans to bring you prosperity and not disaster, plans to bring about the future you hope for." (Jeremiah 29:11).

Zechariah waited for God's blessing with unbelief, like us. God melted his unbelief and loosed his tongue at the naming ceremony of John. During this Christmas are we waiting for God with belief or unbelief? We've looked at the life of Zechariah… *the first person to whom God ever announced his coming into the world.* In many ways, his story is the story of us. During this advent be ready to be part of His melting plan...

Day 4
Melt the frozen wax . . . melt the frozen heart

"When Herod realized that he had been outwitted by the Magi, he was furious, and he gave orders to kill all the boys in Bethlehem and its vicinity who were two years old and under, in accordance with the time he had learned from the Magi" (Matthew 2:16).

Herod – the king frozen with Selfishness

Herod couldn't understand the real meaning of Christmas. Christmas is the lived-out story authored by the creator of life and reality. The creator of tears and laughter, the creator of mountains and valleys. It is a story about being restored to the original purpose for which each of us is intended. It is about the essence under the skin of our lives. But Herod's heart was frozen with selfishness which made him blind. He became ignorant and arrogant

In the gospel of Matthew, everyone responded in different ways to the news of the birth of Jesus. Herod's frozen heart responded in a different way. Herod is concerned with only one thing… preserving his position of power and influence. He is not interested in the truth and its implications for his life. He didn't want to be part of God's great plan and its happiness. He made a mess at Christmas. In an effort to protect his throne and his power, Herod wanted to kill the young King for whom the wise men were looking. Herod symbolizes the selfishness that threatens what is good.

Stealing the happiness

There is a story by Dr Seuss, "How the Grinch stole Christmas". In the story everyone at Who-ville loved Christmas. Everyone, that is, except the Grinch. The Grinch hated Christmas and made up a plan to spoil the joy of Christmas in Who-ville. He planned to dress up as Santa Claus, go into Who-ville and steal all of their Christmas presents, all of their Christmas trees, and even the food for their Christmas dinner. What a terrible thing to do! Do you know why the Grinch hated Christmas so much? Well, according to the story, it was because his heart was too small! He was so selfish that he hated to see anyone else being happy and enjoying themselves. But the Grinch's plan did not work. Why? The Grinch didn't hear what he thought he would hear. He didn't hear weeping and wailing. Instead...he heard singing. The people of Who-ville once again gathered in the square, as is their custom—even without their trees, trimmings, presents and parties – to hold hands and to sing the songs of Christmas. The Grinch might have stolen their temporal things, but he could not steal their Christmas. Because the people in Who-ville knew that the real joy of Christmas did not come from the presents, decorations, and food —it came from a heart filled with love.

The story of "How the Grinch Stole Christmas" is not a true story, but Herod acted like the Grinch in the Christmas story. When we think only of ourselves and act selfishly, we are letting self-interests rule our lives just like Herod. When we are uncomfortable with the truths that the Lord has provided to help us turn from selfishness, we too are opposing the Lord in our lives.

Are we stealing the happiness of this Christmas like Herod? Are we spoiling and messing this Christmas with a selfish mindset? Are we creating happiness or sadness around us? Whether our actions are making us smile or cry? It is time to pause and think about living within the abiding experience in Christ. It is the time to change our frozen hearts; we need to be melted, emptied and purified. Let us pray to God for helping us to melt our hearts.

Day 5
Melt the frozen wax . . . melt the frozen heart

"And she gave birth to her firstborn son and wrapped him in bands of cloth, and laid him in a manger, because there was no place for them in the inn" (Luke. 2:7).

"Sorry, no room in the inn"

Countless times, this phrase paused us. When we are preparing for Christmas, can you remember how many times we said "sorry no room" to our fellow beings? We hang out this signboard to feel safe and protect ourselves against "those people" who don't have a reservation or who are not one of us. There is no reference in the Bible about an innkeeper, but somebody responsible at the inn directed Joseph to the manger. He could have made some alternate arrangement to find a room for the fully pregnant Mary. But his frozen heart was preoccupied, and he didn't realize that he had turned away the world's most important God's chosen couple. This man with a frozen heart had no sympathy for Mary, Joseph and the child Mary was carrying.

Do we feel a piercing pain in the heart? Did we ever feel the pain of being rejected? Mary and Joseph knew what it felt like. Jesus did too. How ironic, given that Jesus spent his entire life doing the opposite — "making room" for everyone around him. In this life we should not forget one thing, we are not here to say "no room", but we are here to "make room for others." Christmas is a time to meditate that the 'other' is a gift from God.

Boy Changed the Script

*Jimmy was in the 8th grade, but because of his mental limitations as a Special Education child, he couldn't do all of the 8th grade work. The teacher in that class planned a Christmas play. Jimmy wanted to be in it very much. The teacher doubted whether he would be able to memorize his lines, but all the students wanted to include Jimmy. So, he was assigned the role of the Bethlehem innkeeper, primarily because that character had only two words to say: "No room." Then after Mary begged for special consideration, he was supposed to say those same words again, "No room." Eventually, the day of the performance came. Lots of families and friends were in the audience. Mary and Joseph approached the inn and knocked on the door. Jimmy opened the door and said flawlessly, "No room." Then Mary said, "But I'm very tired and I'm going to have a baby real soon. If I don't find a safe place for my baby to be born, I'm going to cry." Jimmy paused for a moment, and then said, "I know what I'm supposed to say . . . **but you can have my room.**" Jimmy was willing to violate a script to follow the higher impulse of love.*

No room for God, the loving creator, in our busy, packed, anxious lives. And no small wonder then, that neither do we have much room for those who are the helpless victims in the turbulence of this world. If this has been true for us this year, then Advent offers us a fresh opportunity to make room, think of the Ukrainian refugees. Not only in our own heart for the baby Jesus, but also, in His name, to make room for those who have seen all too often the sign that says position filled, or no vacancies or stay out.

We Christians must be willing to violate the cultural script about Christmas if we want to truly glorify the saviour. We are frozen wax, with prejudiced mindset, selfishness, and self-centeredness. We are busy with our own affairs. We are profit oriented. But during this Christmas while changing the furniture for finding space for the Christmas tree, we need to find some space for our Lord and our fellow beings in our hearts. For that, we need to melt our hearts and make them pure.

Day 6
Melt the frozen wax ... melt the frozen heart

"When King Herod heard this, he was disturbed, and all Jerusalem with him"

(Matthew 2: 3).

"All Jerusalem with Herod" – disturbed with frozen minds

Streets are decorated, people are busy with shopping, buying gifts, Christmas parties . . . in the midst of all these busy schedules, are we missing Jesus Christ? Yesterday it was the innkeeper who missed Christmas. His inn had no room because a census was being held in Bethlehem. Not only his inn, but also his heart was preoccupied. There was still an excuse for him, he didn't know it was the King.

For Jerusalem, the wise men announced the good news to King Herod. They got disturbed thinking about the arrival of a new political king, also they had no space and no time for the long-awaited true Messiah. Jerusalem prayed for a change and they knew the prophecy about Messiah's arrival. When change drew near, they feared. Isn't that a lot like us at times? What if it were announced to us that Jesus Christ is on his way back to earth? How would we react? ***Would we be disturbed***? We pray to God to change things for the better in our lives. But when He starts to bring the changes, we become fearful. The reason is, deep down, we don't want any interruption in the way we are. It happens to us because we are not prioritising Jesus in our lives, and the same thing happened in Jerusalem. The birth of Christ took place only a few miles away. It was the fulfilment of all their dreams and hopes, the event that would change the destiny of the world, but they missed it.

Fill Christ first

One day, an expert in time management was speaking to a group of business students. He pulled out a wide mouthed mason jar and set it on the table in front of him. He also produced some fist-sized rocks and carefully placed them into the jar one by one. When the jar was filled to the top and no more rocks would fit inside, he asked - "Is this jar full?" Everyone in the class shouted, "yes." The expert responded, "Really?" He reached under the table and pulled out a bucket of gravel. He dumped some gravel in and shook the jar causing pieces of gravel to work themselves down into the spaces between the big rocks. He then asked the group once more, "Is the jar full?" By this time the class was on to him. "Probably not," one of them answered. "Good!" he replied. He brought out a bucket of sand. He started dumping the sand in the jar and it went into all of the spaces left between the rocks and the gravel. Once more he asked the question, "Is this jar full?" "No!" the class shouted. Once again, he said, "good." Then he grabbed a pitcher of water and began to pour it in until the jar was filled to the brim. Then he looked at the class and asked, "What is the point of this illustration?" One eager student raised his hand and said, "The point is, no matter how full your schedule is, if you try hard, you can always fit some more things in it!" "No," the speaker replied, "that's not the point. This illustration teaches us: If you don't put the big rocks in first, you'll never get them in at all."

Are we filling the jar with water first, or did we first place our rock Christ in our mind jar? If we leave the most important Christ in our life to the last then this advent will disturb us. We need to melt our hearts to place him first in our hearts. Christmas is a time to focus on His birth and try to understand who He is. He was here to save us not to prosecute us. Instead of having a frozen disturbed mind, we should be melted and filled with the joy of Christmas. O Lord, melt us . . . melt us to fill our hearts with You.

Day 7
Melt the frozen wax . . . melt the frozen heart

"Gathering together all the chief priests and scribes of the people, he began to inquire of them where the Christ was to be born? . . . And they said to him, "In Bethlehem of Judea, for so it has been written by the prophet." (Matthew 2:4 & 5).

Focus of the frozen hearts

Herod asked the right people, the chief priests and scribes to get more information about Christ's birth. The chief priests were the ones who conducted the Temple duties. The scribes were the scholars and the authorities on the Bible. Many of the scribes had memorized the entire Old Testament. They would get a scroll and, with no help, write out the entire Old Testament. They would start at Genesis and inscribe all the way to the end!

They knew when the Messiah would be presented as the King because it was foretold in the Book of Daniel. They knew where He would be born because it was prophesied in the Book of Micah. And these books were included in the Scriptures they laboriously memorized. But why didn't they prepare for the day?

With the knowledge they had of the scriptures, they should have been practically running to find Him. But why didn't they drop everything and go to Bethlehem? Probably because they were busy. Busy with the Temple services, busy with their lecture on Old Testament messianic prophecy, busy being chief priests and scribes. None of this was wrong in itself — but they didn't put the theories into practice. Their focus on these legitimate things made them indifferent to the most important thing, which turned into a full-blown tragedy! They lost the focus on the actual purpose with their frozen hearts.

Neglecting the fellowship with Christ

*"Satan called a worldwide convention. In the opening address to his evil spirits, he said, 'We can't keep true Christians from going to church. We can't keep them from reading their Bibles and knowing the truth. We can't even keep them from having conservative values. But we can do something else. We can keep them away from forming an intimate, abiding experience with Christ. If they gain that connection with Jesus, our power over them will be broken. So let them go to church, read their Bibles, and have their conservative lifestyles, but steal their time so they do not have time to have an intimate fellowship with Christ. This is what I want you to do: **keep them busy** in the non-essentials of life and invent innumerable schemes to occupy their minds.' How tragic it is that the devil has been so successful in getting so many believers to overextend themselves today in this world's pursuits to the neglect of fellowship with Christ!"*

The same thing happened with the priests and scribes; they couldn't identify the purpose of their lives. They never thought about their destinations – eternal life. The result was they lost a fellowship and they missed Christmas. If we are too busy to discover the meaning of our existence and the purpose of our life, too busy to meet God personally and experience His love, then let us take this opportunity to melt ourselves. When it comes to finding God, the most important factor is not only our upbringing or our biblical knowledge — it's our heart's attitude.

If we are willing to admit our need for God and tell Him we want to know Him, He will melt us and make us ready to get moulded and lead us to Jesus. Today, let us make sure we are completely melted and ready to follow the Christmas star.

Day 8
Mash the fragrance . . . mash the fruits

*"But the fruit of the Spirit is love, joy, peace, forbearance,
kindness, goodness, faithfulness, gentleness and self-control"
(Galatians 5:22-23).*

Fruits and Melted heart

During this Advent, we immersed ourselves in the process of turning into the best candles. We are progressing from melting to mashing. We found examples that melted their fear, doubt and unbelief in the fire of God. We also saw people who couldn't melt their frozen hearts, but they missed Christmas. We are prepared not to miss Advent. The echoes of examples made an impact on us and we are melted by Him. Now we don't want to be ordinary candles at the manger, we want to be coloured and fragrant filled with love. So, we are mashing our melted hearts with the fruits of the Holy Spirit. One at a time!

Mashing with Love

Christmas is a great love story of God's **self-giving love, agape**, for mankind. *"For God so loved the world, that he gave his only Son" (John 3:16a)*. God made Christmas to remind us about His Love and how worthy we are. How we can ignore Him and His love! He showed the greatest possibility of love and asked us to follow the greatest commandments of love - Love our God with a full heart and love our neighbours as yourself (Matthew22:37-39). Luke 6:32 explains that it is so easy to love those who love us. There is little effort. But the reward for loving those who do not love us in return or do wrong to us is incredible. Remember, the deal is with God not with people. Let us mash His love into our melted hearts and reflect it to others.

Winning the love

Once upon a time, there was a king who was rich and powerful. He wanted to marry someone whom he could love and who could love him the most. One day the King was riding through the streets of a small village, a remote corner of the kingdom then he saw the most beautiful girl he had ever seen. He immediately fell in love with her. But there was a problem: she was a peasant girl. The problem was that he wanted to win her love, not to buy her love. One of his ministers told him to just command her to be his wife. Any girl would accept the golden opportunity. But the King would not do that. He could not command love. Another minister told the king to call her to the palace and shower her with presents of diamonds and gold. But the King would not do that. For the rest of his life, he would wonder if she loved him or his wealth. A third minister told the king to dress as a peasant so she would not be overwhelmed, and gradually reveal his power and position until she was ready to join him in the castle. The king did not like the thought of deceiving her. If their relationship was based on deception, how could she ever love him? Finally, the King knew what he had to do. He renounced his royal robes, his power and authority. He became a peasant in that remote village, living, working and suffering beside other peasants. After many years, he won the heart of the beautiful young girl.

Do we recognize the King who came from heaven for winning our love? Yes, the baby in the manger. God turned to the man to win our fellowship with Him, at-one-ment. He walked with us, showed us and taught us real love. What we are going to return? Our call is to make His Love a reality for others. To show our love to God, we need to love our fellow beings. *Whoever does not love does not know God, because **God is love*** (1 John4:8). Surrender our hatred and mash our melted heart with love, the love that stretched from manger to the cross.

Day 9
Mash the fragrance . . . mash the fruits

"Do not be afraid; for behold, I proclaim to you good news of great joy that will be for all the people."(Luke 2:10).

Mashing our melted hearts with Joy

During Advent for turning into a fragrance-filled Candle we are mashing our melted heart with the second fruit of the Holy Spirit - Joy. Once Mother Teresa said, *"Joy is prayer; joy is strength; joy is love -* Joy is a net of love *by which you can catch souls. She gives most who gives with joy."* The reverse of that statement also is true - she who gives most knows joy. Joy is a derivative of giving as well as a motivation for giving. Joy is sufficient for all seasons - constant even if silent through an illness, the demise of a son or a daughter, the loss of a relationship, the pain of unemployment, or the disappointment of shattered dreams. Joy is a gift from God within us that is nurtured by belief and sustained in a life patterned after the one whose birth causes us to sing *Joy to the World.* So, whether with smiles spread across our faces or with tears reaming down our faces, we give ourselves to the tasks that help to create the possibility of joy in others. The one chosen by God to give birth to Jesus was found pregnant outside of marriage yet melted her fear and mashed with joy by lifting her voice to God singing "my spirit rejoices." The joy of Mary was not rooted in a self-congratulatory celebration of personal honor but her profound, compassion-driven understanding of the social impact of her son's life.

We cannot find joy by pursuing it. Joy will find us as a derivative of our pursuits. We cannot shop for joy, grab joy, purchase joy, or hold joy so close to our hearts that it is never absent from our lives. Joy is a gift that comes into our lives through the backdoor of our lives as a result of what is moving into us and out of the front door of our lives. The arrival of joy may surprise us but its presence in our lives is obvious to everyone around us.

Joyful Man

An emperor became bed-ridden from frequent episodes of acute depression. A famous physician suggested a radical remedy to cure the condition. He said, "Identify a truly joyful man and borrow his shirt. Let the emperor wear that shirt. He will be cured." Soldiers were sent in different directions to find a joyful man. They searched everywhere but no one was fully satisfied and filled with joy. Everyone had some worries, at least a minor one. One captain, while returning from a remote village, heard a soft and sweet whistling sound. It was from a very poor man. He was stopped and questioned by the captain. He agreed that he did not have any worry and was always merry. He worked hard in a quarry and earned enough every day. He could easily meet his humble needs and find some money to help the needy people around him. The captain disclosed his mission. Hearing the request, the poor man laughed aloud. The captain was confused. The captain repeated his request. The man asked, "How can I give you a shirt, captain? I don't have even a single shirt and I have never worn a shirt in my life!"

With money, we may be able to buy a good bed but not sleep; good books but not wisdom; good food but not appetite; good medicines but not health; costly ornaments but not beauty. True joy is the result of a correct attitude to life. During this Advent, mashing with joy begins in the commitment of our lives to acts of service and the devotion of our lives to the work of creation. Oh Lord, during this mashing help us to remember why you came as a human in this world; with that Joy in our heart, transform us.

Day 10
Mash the fragrance ... mash the fruits

"Glory to God in the highest, and on earth peace to men on whom his favor rests."(Luke 2:14).

Mashing our melted hearts with Peace

Last two days the mashing process has been gently applied to our melted hearts. Today our Lord has picked the fruit of Peace to mash us. Peace - Christmas cards speak about it, and Christmas carols sing about it. Even the angels at Bethlehem proclaimed that *peace on earth* is with those on whom *God's favour* rests.

How is it that *His favour* "rests" on someone? His favour, His grace is available to all humans. This a costly grace. Many are not interested and have no time for God. His favour doesn't rest on them. It has been rejected. However, as soon as one turns to God and accepts Him as Saviour and Lord of their lives, His favour and His grace live upon them. Without a second thought, Shepherds accepted Him and glorified Him. They became men with good will.

What about *Peace*? We all need two kinds of peace in our lives. We need inner peace, but we also need peace with others. God addresses both. He tells us what to do to find inner peace. It begins with a relationship with God, and it continues as we focus on His strength and allow Him to fill us. *"You will keep him in perfect peace whose mind is focused on you because He trusts in You" (Isaiah 26:3)*. We obtain peace with God through faith in Jesus Christ. Peace with others begins as we understand that God has called us to be peacemakers in our world. *"Blessed are the peacemakers for they will be called the children of God" (Matthew 5:9)*. We experience the peace of God as we walk in unity with Christ and with one another. Peace is so much more than just a lack of fighting. Sure, we want that for our world - but the peace that the Bible talks about is so much deeper than that. It's the absence of striving, and quiet confidence in God, even in the *midst* of great conflict.

A perfect picture of Peace

There once was a king who offered a prize to the artist who would paint the best picture of peace. The king looked at all the pictures. But there were only two he liked. One picture was of a calm lake. The lake was a perfect mirror for peaceful towering mountains all around it. Overhead was a blue sky with fluffy white clouds. All who saw this picture thought that it was a perfect picture of peace. The other picture had mountains, too. But these were rugged and bare. Above was an angry sky, from which rain fell and in which lightening played. Down the side of the mountain tumbled a foaming waterfall. This did not look peaceful at all. But when the king looked closely, he saw behind the waterfall a tiny bush growing in a crack in the rock. In the bush, a mother bird had built her nest. There, in the midst of the rush of angry water, sat the mother bird on her nest - in perfect peace. Which picture do you think won the prize? The king chose the second picture. Do you know why? "Because," explained the king, "peace does not mean to be in a place where there is no noise, trouble, or hard work. Peace means to be in the midst of all those things and still be calm in your heart. That is the real meaning of peace."

"Peace on earth" is all about the very attitudes of our hearts; it is a way of life more than a cute seasonal phrase. Our words convey the attitude of our hearts and create either a culture of peace or culture of hate within our homes. Like Shepherds, we can accept Him without using our logical thinking and melt our hearts to be mashed with His peace, so that we will be filled with the heavenly fragrance of peace.

Day 11
Mash the fragrance . . . mash the fruits

"Be completely humble and gentle; be patient, bearing with one another in love" (Ephesians 4:2).

Mashing our melted hearts with Forbearance

During this Advent when we are mashing with forbearance, we need to keep in mind we are celebrating the birth of the greatest forbearer in the whole world. The Greek word for "forbear" is also defined as "to bear with" or "give slack to". Forbearance goes against that which is natural within the human psyche. In forbearance, we give people the room to be uniquely themselves without a spirit of disapproval or judgment. It sounds simple, but in a world of snap judgments and hyper-criticism, forbearance is very difficult. Our king of Kings born at Bethlehem showed the greatest path of forbearance through His crucifixion. His birth in the manger pointed us to the highest level of humbleness.

Throughout His life journey, He successfully placed the thought of forbearance into the mind of His disciples. On His way to Jerusalem, an entire Samaritan village refused to accommodate Him and His disciples only because they were Jews. This infuriated the two brothers, James and John, who consequently asked Jesus if they should call fire down from

41

heaven on that Samaritan village, just as Elijah had once done upon a band of enemy soldiers. They felt the Samaritans should die for their offence. Jesus rebuked both brothers for their attitude and said, *"You don't realize what your hearts are like. For the Son of Man has not come to destroy men's lives, but to save them."* (Luke 9:55-56). This Christmas, we should mash our melted hearts with this level of forbearance.

Act of Forbearance

A rich man bought a young slave from the market to work in his farm. The slave was a Christian and obeyed his master's orders with love and respect. Impressed by his innocence and dedication, the landowner asked him to accompany him during his next visit to the slave market to buy more slaves for his new farms. Reaching the slave market, they saw a large number of slaves displayed for sale. The owner sought the opinion of the slave in selecting suitable slaves. The slave pointed at an old and frail man and pleaded to purchase him. The rich man was reluctant as the man was old and weak, but the young slave insisted. Finally, the old man was bought and brought to the farm. The young slave was eager to help the old slave and even shared his duties with pleasure. When he fell ill, the young slave looked after him and saved him with his tender care. Seeing these acts of affection, the master asked the young slave whether the old man was his father or a close relative. The young slave denied it. When the master insisted, he told the story of his association with the old man. When the young slave was a child, the old man had stolen him and sold him as a slave to the slave traders. The master asked, "That means he is your worst enemy. Then why did you care for him?" The young slave replied, "Sir, I am a Christian. Jesus taught us to love our enemies. I am following His commandments." The owner was impressed by this exemplary display of Christian love. He became a true Christian and granted freedom to his slaves.

By faith, we can model God's great patience towards those who disturb or deeply disappoint us. During this Advent, we should follow His example and show forbearance to others. We are sinners, too, so why should we point out the tiny speck when we carry a beam of sin ourselves? *"Love covers all transgressions" (Proverbs 10:12b)*. At this Christmas, may our Lord mash our melted heart with the fruit of forbearance, let us rather love one another than condemn without facts.

Day 12
Mash the fragrance . . . mash the fruits

"Mary stayed with Elizabeth for about three months and then returned home" (Luke 1:56).

Mashing with the fruit of Kindness

C hristmas is near; we are preparing ourselves for the great day with the help of our Lord. While mashing is in progress, we can choose to fan anger or fuel kindness; we can be concerned only about ourselves or we can care compassionately about others. The Advent begins with the annunciation of the angle of John the Baptist (Luke 1: 5-25). Then we can see a young girl after her talk with the angel travelling to Judea to see an old lady. She went there to affirm her belief and Mary knew that, at that stage, no one else other than Elizabeth could understand the miracle behind her pregnancy.

Elizabeth was the first to recognize the awesome role, and indeed burden placed on Mary who was to become the mother of God. Elizabeth was kind enough to accept Mary. Would we be happy to give shelter to an unmarried pregnant relative? We should not forget one more thing, Elizabeth was the wife of a priest, and both of them were keeping all the laws of God. But Elizabeth was very kind, she took the risk. For three months it was Elizabeth's fire that warmed the young mother of Jesus,

Elizabeth's roof that kept her dry, and Elizabeth's food that nurtured the tiny child beginning to grow within Mary. In return, for these three months, Elizabeth's house was blessed by the hidden presence of The Messiah. Kindness doesn't just flow out of our lives effortlessly. It has to be worked at, nourished, and encouraged. It takes effort to be kind to people because it often means going out of our way to be nice when it would be easier not to be nice. The priest and Levite wondered *"What will happen to me if I help?"* while the Samaritan wondered *"What will happen to the man if I don't help?"* that question gave him the name **Good Samaritan**.

Two Wolves fighting

A five-year-old boy is sent to spend the summer with his grandfather, who is a respected tribal elder. The boy adores his grandfather and observes his every move. Soon he notices a pattern. Every morning at sunrise, the grandfather goes to the altar in his home, removes a necklace, and places it on the altar. Then he sits in silence for a few minutes. Afterwards, he puts on the necklace and continues with his day. Each evening at sunset the grandfather repeats the same ritual. After a few days, the curious youth asks his grandfather what he is doing. "I am taking some time to quiet my spirit and honour our ancestors, the older man replies. "But what is on the necklace?", his grandson asks. Taking it off, he shows it to the boy who sees the heads of two wolves. "Grandfather, what does it mean?" "Well," the grandfather replies, "Inside of each of us, there are two wolves fighting to control us. One of them is scared and mean and has a hunger that can never be filled. It cares only about itself. The other is brave and kind and shares whatever it has with others. It cares as much about the community as it does for itself." Amazed and somewhat frightened by those symbols, the boy asks, "Grandfather, which wolf will win?" The elder smiles at his grandson and replies, "Whichever one we feed the most."

Practising kindness and compassion is one of the most powerful contributions any of us can make to our family, our community, and our world. People who embrace the power of kindness will find themselves living better lives. Their words and deeds of kindness will be self-transforming and will elevate and transform the lives of all those who they encounter. Oh Lord, mash us with your kindness; help us to be kind to others. During this Christmas, we are submitting our melted hearts for mashing with kindness.

Day 13
Mash the fragrance . . . mash the fruits

"No one is good except God alone" (Mark 10:18).

Mashing with the fruit of Goodness

Today we are giving our melted hearts to be filled with goodness. We cannot describe goodness with words. But we know that God is good and He created us in His image. So, we inherited goodness which we lost in Eden. But God had a purpose for us. So, he created a plan and its first step was Christmas. It is a story about God's goodness and His love. When we hear the carols and see the lights around us, we should realize that this Christmas is the melting, mashing, moulding plan for us by God. The spotlight is on us, He is looking at us. We are really important to Him; we are valuable to Him. He needs us-for establishing the kingdom values on the earth

Character of Goodness

In the Dennis the Menace cartoon, you know that Dennis is a perpetual menace to his next-door neighbours, Mr. and Mrs. Wilson. And yet Mrs. Wilson continues to be kind and gracious to Dennis. One cartoon shows Dennis and his friend Joey leaving Mrs. Wilson's house, their hands full of cookies.

Joey asks, "I wonder what we did to deserve this?" Dennis tells his friend, "Joey, Mrs. Wilson gives us cookies not because we're nice, but because she's nice." Dennis is spot-on; Mrs. Wilson's actions were not about Dennis and Joey, they were about her. She acted out of her character of kindness and goodness.

We can see God in this story. Here, He gave us Christmas instead of cookies. In the book *Original Blessing* by theologian *Mathew Fox*, he says, our birth itself is an original blessing. Although it is indeed evil and sin in the world, it is not because we can't help ourselves. Rather it is because we've become fundamentally separated from our true nature, which is good, not evil that happened at Eden. Goodness is a perspective that affirms creation as good, which sees the beauty of all life. It recognizes the sanctity, the holiness of all life. Holiness would be an appropriate synonym for goodness. It is a way of walking and working in the world that treats everything and every being with respect and reverence. The quality of goodness or holiness makes Christians distinctive in the way they do business, relate to others, their attitude toward the poor, the way we use money, and the priorities we set for our living. During Christmas, we need to remember and embrace our inherited goodness from God. Our original calling is to treat others with goodness and kindness.

The best time to practice goodness is Christmas. We can't go about measuring goodness by what we don't do, but by what we deny ourselves and by what we resist. We've got to measure goodness by what we embrace, what we create, and who we include. To say he or she is a good man or a woman does not do justice to the depth of the fruit of goodness. It puts too much emphasis on the human element in being good. Goodness comes from God to do good for God.

During this advent, we need to understand we are an original blessing of God, created in the very image of God. Our true nature is goodness. May we reclaim the goodness within us during this Advent time. *"With this in mind, we constantly pray for you, that our God may make you worthy of his calling, and that by his power he may bring to fruition your every desire for goodness and your every deed prompted by faith"* *(2 Thess1:11)*. May the fragrance of our God-given goodness fill the manger at Bethlehem.

Day 14
Mash the fragrance . . . mash the fruits

"Teach me your way, LORD, that I may rely on your faithfulness; give me an undivided heart, that I may fear your name" (Psalm 86:11).

Mashing with the fruit of Faithfulness

Each time when Christmas comes, we may resolutely proclaim ourselves that we will be committed to God; from this Christmas onwards, we will be faithful to God's will and so on. But, how long does that commitment last? Faithfulness is a matter of trust, commitment, of fidelity. Last few days when we were mashed with the fruits of the Holy Spirit. Once when we experienced the preceding fruit of the Spirit: the joy of participating in the activity of God, the awe of patiently suffering with others, and the honour of offering acts of kindness and goodness, we are inspired to be faithful.

We are living in a world of so many options that it is often tempting for people to renege on faithfulness. We may sign on for a service, but when a better offer comes along, we'll switch loyalties without a thought of the previous commitment made to a relationship or employer. And we say "Let's move on". Evelyn Underhill writes, "Faithfulness means continuing quietly with the job we have been given, in the situation where we have been placed; not yielding to the restless desire for change. It means tending the lamp quietly for God without wondering how much longer it has got to go on."1

Jesus calls us to live in faithfulness – here, now, in this place, at this moment – in this season of Advent. Remember, we are not prognosticators of the faith but practitioners of the faith.

Expecting the master today

A lovely villa rests on the shores of beautiful Lake Como in the Italian Alps. Some tourists complimented the trusted old gardener who had maintained the grounds for years.

"The owner must come here frequently," one said.

"No," he replied. "He was here only once in 15 years, and then I did not see him."

"But how do you get your orders?"

"From the owner's agent, who lives in Milan."

"Then he must come here often?"

"No, not often. Perhaps once a year or so."

The tourist was amazed. "You have no one to supervise your work, and the grounds are so neat as if you expected the owner to come back tomorrow!"

The old gardener firmly replied, "Today, sir! Not tomorrow, but today!" That gardener was faithful to his trust.

We were unfaithful to our God from the beginning, so we lost the garden. Then 2000 years before on a Christmas day, He sent His only son to us to get us back. He cleansed our sins and gave us a new life. We are expecting Him back, but are we prepared enough? Are we faithful enough? With a wealth of opportunities at our fingertips, as followers of Christ, it is important to be mindful of our core commitments, practice fidelity, be loyal, and be true to our word. While mashing our melted heart with the fruit of faithfulness that is pondering these questions in us. We can be faithful to Him, He is ready to wipe our tears, and He is ready to accept our mistakes. He understands us better than anyone. He knows our shortcomings. Let's surrender ourselves with hands up and heart down, Oh Lord, mash us . . . mash us with faithfulness.

Day 15
Mash the fragrance . . . mash the fruits

"Rejoice in the Lord always. I will say it again: Rejoice!
Let your gentleness be evident to all. The Lord is near."
(Philippians 4:4-5).

Mashing with the fruit of Gentleness

Yes, our Lord is nearby. He is in the Manger waiting for us. We are on a journey. In this journey, our Lord is mashing us with the right fragrances to turn into the right candle at Bethlehem. The definition of gentleness is "power under control," The pictures of a horse under control, water in a reservoir . . . God on the cross talks about gentleness. Who could provide us with a better example of gentleness and humility than Jesus himself?

As we see baby Jesus in the manger, we reflect on God's way is as a way of gentleness. God's way is not one of violence, but gentleness. There is a lack of goodness and love in the world, but God is tender and loving. As we look at baby Jesus in the manger, we see that he is the answer to today's problems. Instead of violence, in baby Jesus in the manger we see gentleness. Instead of hatred, in baby Jesus in the manger we see tenderness. Instead of selfishness, in baby Jesus in the manger we see love for us. Let us ask baby Jesus to help us to be gentle, tender and loving with those around us as he was in the manger. Gentleness is difficult for us because it feels like weakness. Gentleness is not weakness. It is not allowing ourselves to become a doormat. It is part of God's character as He moves triumphantly in mighty power and victory. So, it is time to mash our melted hearts with gentleness shown by the baby in the manger.

Gentleness and Power

On one occasion, George Washington was fox hunting with a group of friends. One of the fields through which they were passing was bordered by a stone wall. As his horse jumped the wall it knocked off a stone. Washington immediately stopped, got down from his horse, and replaced the stone. One of his friends said, "You are too big a man to bother with that." He replied gently, "No, I am just the right size." There is another story tells of a corporal at Valley Forge who was directing three men as they tried to lift a log into place. It was too heavy, but the corporal commanded again and again, "All right, men, one, two, three, lift!" A man in an overcoat came by and said to the corporal, 'Why don't you help them?" The corporal pulled himself up to full height and replied, "Sir, I am a corporal." Without a word, the man stepped over and with his help, the log went easily into place. The man was George Washington.

Gentleness is never self-important but is considerate, courteous, and modest, yet willing to try when a job needs to be done. The Bible says Moses excelled in meekness that is gentleness (Numbers 12:3). God gave him a high position. It is hard for the natural man to be gentle toward those who attack him, especially if they attack his official rank and honour. But Moses showed gentleness. Jesus knew who He was, but He was gentle. Jesus' awareness of His power enabled Him to be gentle to those in need.

During Christmas, we are getting the opportunity to mash with gentleness. We can't pretend to be gentle or pretend to have an open heart, it won't work. This gentleness is cultivated through practice. It's like a muscle - the more we use it the stronger it gets. What a grace it is that we have the opportunity and that allows us to practice this open-heart gentleness. During this Advent, we should be able to give unconditional gentleness, unconditional hugs, and unconditional smiles to the people in need. May our Lord help us today to be filled with gentleness.

Day 16
Mash the fragrance . . . mash the fruits

"For the grace of God has appeared that offers salvation to all people. It teaches us to say "No" to ungodliness and worldly passions, and to live self-controlled, upright and godly lives in this present age, while we wait for the blessed hope—the appearing of the glory of our great God and Savior, Jesus Christ." (Titus 2:11-13).

Mashing with the fruit of Self-Control

Christmas undoubtedly has all the ingredients for a joyful celebration – the opportunity to be with family and friends and exchange gifts – but, Christmas can also strain our self-control and tolerance. This Christmas while journeying to Bethlehem we need to be mashed with self-control along with other fruit of the Spirit. Interestingly, it is very difficult to finish our mashing without self-control. Can we love well if our temper is out of control? Can we have true joy if we allow our flesh to be out of control? We surely can't have peace if we have no self-control, let alone forbearance, kindness, goodness, faithfulness and gentleness. Mashing of all these fruits works only in a self-controlled life.

Again Jesus Christ is the man who showed to us the real meaning of self-control. He showed his self-control to Satan when He was in the desert. The next one is the old Testament figure, Joseph. His answer to Potiphar's wife was "How then could I do such a wicked thing and sin against God?". Most of the time when we say some bad words or do some bad deeds we look left and right and make sure no one else heard or saw that, but we forget to look up. But Joseph looked up and saw God and he had the fear of God. Today our temptations might not be similar to Joseph's but, our answer needs to be the same as his, then only we can say we are mashed with self-control. Christmas distracts us a lot with presents, shows, gathering, parties. Nothing is wrong but, we should give our control to God.

Distractions Stealing our Destinations

A man went to the airport. While waiting for his flight, he spotted a machine that said, "Insert a coin, step on the plate, and I'll say your name and your destination." The man was very curious, so he put in a coin and stood on the machine. The screen lit up and a message appeared: "Your name is Peter Smith and your destination is New York." Peter Smith was astonished and very impressed. He could not resist testing the machine again, so he put in another coin. The same message appeared. How could a mere machine know his name and where he was going? He was so fascinated that he put in another coin, but received the same result. He tried the machine many times. It never let him down. As he came to his last coin, he stepped on the machine, and it told him: "Your name is Peter Smith and your destination was New York—but, you've just missed your flight." A lot of things in life are tempting. But our desire to indulge needs managing, or what appeared to be enjoyable can turn into a disaster. The difference between a pleasant evening and a state of drunkenness is self-control.

Self-control means remaining in control of our attitudes, thoughts, desires and habits—so they don't overwhelm us and dictate our behaviour. As Peter Smith discovered to his cost, what matters is our destination—but we won't get there unless we remain focused on what's important. While waiting during this Christmas we should be completely focused on Jesus. Today our mashing is complete. For the journey to Bethlehem, this mashing is important, if we don't complete that, we cannot be the right candle at the Manger. Our Lord is ready to mash us; all He needs is a melted heart. Let's melt and give our hearts to him. May He purify us and mash us . . ..

Day 17
Moulding the wax ... moulding the heart

". . . your heavenly Father is perfect." (Matthew 5:48).

God choosing our perfect mould

Our God mashed our melted heart with all fragrance and fruits of the Holy Spirit. We are near Bethlehem. We can see the star in the sky that still shines which we are chasing from the day we decided for melting. Our body is renewed by the fruit of the Spirit. Now we are going to be poured into a mould. The mould was chosen by our God. At this point, if we leave God and give control to the world, the world will squeeze us into its mould, when we bow down to its pressure it takes away our purpose in life.

God is at work melting, mashing, moulding, and doing exactly as He chooses. But He gave us choices at Eden, the choice of leaving him and running, which we always do. The great thing is that when we allow God to mould and shape our lives, He will turn us into wonderful works of art. Like the skilled potter makes a beautiful vase or bowl; so, God makes a beautiful life and a useful life out of a person who is yielded to Him.

God is Perfect

Once there was an atheist, who usually made comments about God. One day while he was travelling from one place to another, he felt weak and tired after a long walk. He rested under a banyan tree for a while. Looking up, he saw tiny fruits on the tall tree. In the adjacent field, he saw large watermelons on a feeble creeper plant. He laughed at the contradiction and thought that God was foolish to grow the small fruits on the strong and tall tree and the large fruits on the weak creeper. After a while, he fell asleep under the cool shade of the huge evergreen tree. Then a small fruit from the tall tree fell on his body and awakened him. Staring at the tiny fruit, he felt enlightened. He thought, "If the fruits of this tree were large like the watermelon, they would have easily crushed me to death. Later in the story, he encountered many such events and realized the existence of God.

"I praise you because I am fearfully and wonderfully made ... " *(Psalm 139:14).* God is the perfect moulder spiritually and physically. The stars, the sky, the mountains everything wonders us. God gives the best and most appropriate gifts, qualities and capabilities to every creation including humans. God has clear plans for each of us. God's plans bring us prosperity and not a disaster.

We are made by God in His image. But, because of our sin, we lost that perfect image. How can we turn into perfect candles. He made Christmas for us as the beginning of our restoration plan. God's purpose is not to perfect us to make us a trophy in His showcase; He is getting us perfect to the place where He can use us. How many times we have failed because we tried to mould the world in our own image. We forgot that the perfect plan is in the hands of God. If we want to understand how God is moulding us, we have to think of Peter in the Bible. He denied Jesus before His crucifixion and said he didn't even know him. It says he wept bitterly when he realized how he had failed the Lord. He must have felt that his relationship with the Lord was over. Peter experienced total brokenness. But then Jesus met him again at the breakfast on the seashore after His resurrection (John 21). In His gentle and loving way, He called Peter back and healed his brokenness, giving him a new assignment to feed his sheep. Our perfect God won't leave us. He corrects our imperfections because He has a perfect mould for each of us. Let Him put our melted hearts into His chosen mould because we don't want to be moulded by the world, we want to be God-made Christians.

Day 18
Moulding the wax . . . moulding the heart

.......and they will call him Immanuel" (which means "God with us") - Mathew 1:23b.

Wick in the Candle . . . Wick in our life

We are getting near to Bethlehem. The chandler arranged the mould. Before pouring, He is arranging the wick. A candle is meaningful when the wick is present. It is the centre and core of it all, the thing that makes it all work. Christmas gives a different twist to the story; **Here Chandler is the wick.** He himself is getting inside the mould and ready to reside in us. Angels are pouring our melted hearts mashed with the fragrances of the Holy Spirit into the mould. He is neither above nor below, He is within us. It is not a fairy story; this is the reality. Christmas whispers to us "I am with you, my child". What a great privilege. We are no more just frozen wax, we are not just wax, we are going to be meaningful candles. That is Christmas. Our core, our centre is God, who runs through us and gives us life.

That's all I want

A well-known minister stood before a Sunday school gathering of small children and asked, "How many of you can quote Psalm 23?" *Several of the children raised their hands, among them a beautiful little blonde-headed girl who could not have been much more than four years old. The pastor was surprised that such a young person would know Psalm 23. So, he asked her to come to the front of the room to recite it for the class. Standing before the class with hands clutched behind her back, the young girl smiled, and the minister smiled back. Then, with great confidence, she said only this: "The Lord is my shepherd. **That's all I want.** " The little girl had the words mixed up, but she got the message right.*

What a beautiful interpretation. Christmas reminds us to say this. He is with us to feel us, He is everything for us. He can change our meaningless lives into meaningful ones. We need to say the same words as that little girl, we need only our Lord. He needs to be our centre, say it louder, don't think of the people around us or where we are, while reading this, and say loudly. *"The Lord is my Center, that's all I want",* that proclamation can change something in our minds. God Himself in human flesh. He valued the relationship with us. With His relationship, He is addressing the loneliness of our hearts. We are living in a world of loneliness, that's why Psalmist says. *"There is no one who takes notice of me; no refuge remains to me; no one cares for me;" (Psalm 142:4).* And it is particularly during the Christmas holidays that loneliness becomes unbearable for many.

Number of years ago, In the questionnaire, a schoolboy answered the question

Why are so many twins born into the world today?

"I believe it is because little children are afraid of entering the world alone".

Christmas is a commitment from God. It is a name in which God commits himself to be our twin… forever; to be with us… always. Immanuel—that name sums up the heart of the gospel.

God with us, the name that brings comfort and caution. For if God is with us, all the time and everywhere, how then are we to act? When a family member hurts us? When a neighbour insults us? When a nation threatens us? If God is with us, what are we to do when we've let a brother or sister in Christ letdown? When we've wronged a friend? When we've angered a colleague? Let us remember with joy and purpose, that God - the Wonderful Counselor, the Prince of Peace is within us . . . the wick of our life.

Day 19
Moulding the wax . . . moulding the heart

"He was waiting for the consolation of Israel, and the Holy Spirit was on him." Luke 2: 25b

Waiting... Waiting for the purpose...

Angels put us into the mould because chandler is now within us. We are in the mould, with God as our centre and filled with the fruits of the Holy Spirit. Now we have the picture of perfection. In the mould we are waiting with God, to become the right candles. He helped us to reach this far. Now we need to wait. Advent itself means waiting. He keeps promises, in His way, in His own time; but He asks us to wait. He promises us, that He will return. He promises to come into our hearts. He promises us pleasant surprises. All we need to do is wait upon the Lord patiently.

Simeon waited for a lifetime

"It had been revealed to him (to Simeon) by the Holy Spirit that he would not see death before he had seen the Lord's Messiah." (Luke 2:26). God promised Simeon that he would not see death before he saw the Messiah, and God kept the promise. Simeon greeted the infant Saviour on the occasion of His presentation in the Temple. "Just wait," is not a favourite phrase

of this world. But Simeon spent a lifetime of waiting for seeing the Messiah. Our impatient generation's vocabulary is filled with words like instant, fast and quick. Whether it is technology, money, food or service, we don't want to wait. Christmas encourages us to "wait upon the Lord." Simeon did a special kind of waiting. Simeon's waiting is creating another thought in us, We are not ready to die until we have embraced Jesus Christ as our Lord and Savior. We may be ready to graduate, we may be ready to buy our first home, we may be ready to retire, we may be ready to do many things—but, friend, without Jesus, We are not ready to die. During the waiting, we need to "wait with hope," not "wait and see what happens." It is not just the passing of time. It is anticipation. In the mould, we have God's promises to anticipate.

Waiting doesn't mean doing anything

Sue Monk Kidd tells a story that reflects our often-mistaken viewpoint on waiting. During a retreat at a monastery, in her restless state, she noticed a monk. He was sitting perfectly still beneath a tree. There was such reverence in his silhouette, such tranquil sturdiness, that she paused to watch. He was the picture of waiting. Later She sought him out. She asked the monk "How is it that you can wait so patiently at the moment? I can't seem to get used to the idea of doing nothing." He broke into a wonderful grin. 'Well, there's the problem right there, young lady. You've bought into the cultural myth that when you're waiting, you're doing nothing." Then he took his hands and placed them on her shoulders, peered straight into her eyes and said, "I hope you'll hear what I'm about to tell you. I hope you'll hear it down to your toes. When you're waiting, it may seem you're not doing anything but you're doing the most important something that is, you're allowing your soul to grow up. If you can't be still and wait, you can't become what God created you to be." "Be still and know that I am God" (Psalm46;10).

While waiting we need our souls to grow up. We should wait patiently. We should believe that He cares for us. When we wait it seems all we're doing is standing around getting nothing accomplished. However, if you read in the gospels, what Jesus will be expecting, when He returns, from the servant who is watching for his return. He showed the correct attitude of waiting by telling the ten virgins' parable. There is only one way to watch. ***It is through patience and preparation to wait.*** Simeon was waiting for the consolation of Israel. And we have a great advantage over Simeon. He saw the baby Messiah but we saw the resurrection. We went through His plans many times. But this time, He is with us in the mould. When this Advent finishes, He has a plan for us.

Oh Lord, You keep Your promises, but even though we believe You are true to Your word, we sometimes grow impatient. Please forgive us, and please strengthen our faith in You. By Your grace may we be so sure of Your faithfulness that we will have no difficulty in waiting for as long as You ask us to wait for settling ourselves with you in the mould.

Day 20
Moulding the wax . . . moulding the heart

"Are you the one who was to come, or should we expect someone else?"(Luke 7:19).

Waiting offends us with questions and fills our doubts.

Yesterday Simeon could identify the true Messiah because of his patience and preparation to wait. When we wait, we often ask questions, are we waiting for the right one? The same doubt was with the very righteous man in the New Testament. Because he had an inherited doubt from Zechariah, that resulted in the above question. Jesus declared John the Baptist to be the greatest man to have ever lived: *"I tell you, among those born of women there is no one greater than John . . . "* The greatest recognition in the world. John the Baptist realized Jesus is the son of God during Jesus' baptism. (John 1:33,34). But when he was in jail, John was expecting Jesus to come and rescue him from prison with His wondrous display of supernatural power. But, instead of moving in that direction, when Jesus came to know of John's imprisonment, He moved farther away! *Now when Jesus had heard that John was cast into prison, he departed into Galilee. (Mat 4:12).*

Our God surprises us. John asked himself. If He was the Messiah, then why was He still humbly walking the land and not assuming regal power? But if He were not, then how could He be doing these miracles? But John didn't understand our Lord came to establish a kingdom greater than any earthly kingdom and to accomplish salvation greater than any earthly deliverance. When we are in the mould, we too can become impatient, we might have some plans about ourselves, we believe that if we are righteous we don't need to undergo this melting, mashing and moulding phase in this advent. We feel it is time consuming, with a simple clap He can turn us into beautiful candles. Our mind may ask the question, why did God turn to man to deliver us? Jesus was reminding John of the ways and approach of God that is so much different from man's finite approach. Christ gently rebukes his forerunner with a blessing intact in it. He said: *Blessed is he, whosoever shall not be offended in me: (Mat 11:6).* God will reveal the purpose to the world, we should not be offended.

Answers for the Christmas questions.

A man who couldn't accept Jesus, about God coming to earth as a man, didn't accompany his wife to church for the Christmas Service. He said he would like to stay at home in the night. Shortly after the family drove away in the car, while reading the newspaper inside the house he was startled by a thudding sound. He went to the front door to investigate; he found a flock of birds in the snow. They had been caught in the storm and a desperate search for shelter had made them try to fly through his large landscape window. Well, he couldn't let the poor creatures lie there and freeze, so he remembered the barn where his children stabled their pony. Quickly, he put on a coat and went outside. He opened the doors wide and turned on a light. But the birds did not come in. He figured food would entice them in. So, he hurried back to the house, fetched breadcrumbs, and sprinkled them on the snow making a trail the yellow lighted, wide-open door to the stable. But to his dismay, the birds ignored the breadcrumbs and continued to flop around helplessly in the snow. They ignored him. Then he realized that they were afraid of him. To them, he reasoned, "I am a strange and terrifying creature. I need to let them know that they can trust me I'm not trying to hurt them but to help them, but how?" Because any move he made tended to frighten them and confuse them. "If only I could be a bird", he thought to himself "and mingle with them and speak their language, then I could tell them not to be afraid". At that moment the church bells began to ring. The sound reached his ears above the sounds of the wind. He stood there listening to the bells and realized why God made Christmas.

During this advent, we may ask the same questions as John the Baptist. Sometimes the world around us asks questions. In this mould let us wait, when someone offends us, let us be calm. We don't need to get victory in front of man because there is a God, who values our heart and its intentions. When we are calm, people say we are acting. But don't forget there is a God, who values everyone. In the mould, in the silence, we feel loneliness like John in the Jail, we doubt about this Christmas, but don't force ourselves to come out of the mould because we may end up with cracks. The world questions our actions, but we don't need to answer. Their questions will turn them into the right candles. Pray inside the mould, so that dream of the chandler will not be shattered.

Day 21
Mirror time ... moulded candles ... moulded hearts

Moulded Candles and Mirror

L ast few weeks we melted our hearts, mashed with fruits of the Holy Spirit and waited in the mould to settle with God. Today we are out of the mould. What we do first; is it to see the change we rush in front of the mirror. Yes, we want to see ourselves. We need to see where we can place ourselves in the Advent wreath. The advent wreath has five candle spaces. Each represents hope, love, joy, peace and Christ candle. The wreath's circle reminds us of God Himself, His eternity and His endless mercy, with no beginning or end. The green speaks of the hope that we have in God, the hope of renewal, of eternal life. The four outer candles represent the waiting period during the four Sundays of Advent, which themselves symbolize the four centuries of waiting between the prophet Malachi and the birth of Christ. Let us see in the mirror what we are ... Everyone looks different because we are made differently for different purposes.

Angels in the mirror

"Do not be afraid. I bring you good news ...." (Luke 2:10a).

If we see angels in the mirror, it means that we have turned into a *candle of Joy* after completing all these phases. Yes, we are like the angels, carriers of joy and good news this Christmas. As a candle of joy, we have great responsibilities. We should make sure, that when we are lighted by Jesus, we should fill the fragrance of joy in this world like the angels. The angles came to proclaim the joyful message of peace for all people that Christ came to save us from our sins. Angels see things from God's point of view. Gabriel's behaviour toward Mary and Zachariah shows that they aren't fooled by a person's pious exterior or impressed by one's high position. Angel's presence should remove people from fear. With our presence, we should be able to say, "*do not be afraid*". The angel in the mirror reminds us that, we are the candles of Joy, so we have the responsibility to take off the fear of the world through our actions. Angels in the nativity story took the fear of Mary and Shepherds and they were guided by the plan of God. The good news in the Bible is given to the people by Angels. Angels make people joyful. So, this Christmas, we have the great responsibility of helping one another. Then only we can grow the Joy of Christmas in us.

We need each other

A boy visited a pet store to purchase a puppy. He was shown different varieties of pet puppies. But he selected a weak, lame and limping puppy lying alone in a corner. The manager explained that it was handicapped, but the boy showed him his crutches which he had to use as support during walking. He said, "That poor, little puppy needs me, and I need him. We need each other."

This Christmas, we need to pass the Joy in us to the needy ones around us. When we say we are perfect now, we should not forget our frozen state in the beginning. Let us pass our perfect joy to others. When we care for people around us and pass the Joy of Christmas, we can step into Bethlehem as a candle of Joy.

Lord, thank you for turning us into candles of Joy! May our actions bring joy to others, especially to all who feel harassed and dejected. May they hear an unspoken greeting: "Fear not, the Lord is with you!". Grant us, Lord, an attentive mind, and heart like angels and help us to comfort the needy with Your words.

Day 22
Mirror time ... moulded candles ... moulded hearts

Yesterday, some of us identified ourselves as the angels, the candles of joy. We are made for making people joyful around us. We were melted, mashed and moulded to take out the fear from people around us with the words of God. Let's see what appears in the mirror today.

Shepherds in the Mirror

"Now there were in the same country shepherds living out in the fields,

keeping watch over their flock by night" (Luke 2: 8).

If we see Shepherds in the mirror, it means all their faces changed us into *candles of love*. We all know that Christmas is the story of God's love. Rather than announcing this important news to the influential people of Israel, God instead chose to reveal this great truth to humble shepherds who occupied one of the lowest rungs on the ladder of the Jewish society.

Why did He choose the Shepherds? The ones who can love their dump sheep and keep them out of the dangers will pass the love of God to the people around them. The second point is, that God wanted the lowliest of humanity to realize that His love included them, especially in a world where they were normally excluded. God chose those people, especially those who are humble, lowly and ordinary to make His power and wisdom all the more evident. When He uses people who are very gifted and powerful, then the results can be attributed to human effort and human talent. There we forget God and follow the world. God chooses to take the "lowest of the low" and bring them into the spotlight, lift them and make them shine, that is the history and the future of God's Kingdom. Shepherds were neither wise nor mighty. *But they excelled at feeding ..gathering...carrying and leading the flock.* The final point is that they were instantly ready to follow the signs of God. In a worldly view, it is foolish to leave the comfort zone and risk their life for seeking God at midnight. We always think about the logical side of an event, but they just followed. For feeling the love of God and passing the love in this Christmas we need to be fools for Christ. Paul describes himself as a fool for Christ. ***Our dedication to Christ makes us look like fools*, as** *1 Corinthians 4:10 describes it.* Paul isn't insulting us with the use of this word, rather he is saying that God's way of thinking and doing is not the world's way. And when you choose a path in life that is off the beaten path of the crowd, we will be branded as fools. This Christmas, let's risk our time to pass His love to the world.

Most loving Child

Once there was a contest to find the most loving child. The winner was a four-year-old child whose next-door neighbour was an elderly gentleman who lost his wife recently. Upon seeing the man cry, the little boy went into the old gentleman's yard, climbed onto his lap, and just sat there. When his mother asked what he had said to the neighbour, the little boy said, "Nothing, I just helped him cry."

In this world, the greatest thing which we can do in love is not the gifts which we are wrapping on Christmas days. It is the time which we can spend with our fellow beings. Let this transformation help us to propagate his love for a lifetime. When we walk with shepherds to Bethlehem, remember that He transformed us into **Candles of love.** When we are the light, we need to pass the love of our God to others.

Oh Lord, Oh Lord, you changed me to a candle of love,
While exciting things occurred all over the world.
Nothing ever happened to me.
Sometimes, I wondered if You know I exist
If You did, I was certain You forgotten where.
But You found me in the darkness, made a plan for me.
Melted, Mashed and Moulded
Now you placed me in front of the mirror
Your love made me and gave me this new image.
Let me help to pass Your love when You light me at Bethlehem

Day 23
Mirror time . . . moulded
candles . . . moulded hearts

Last two days the mirror reflected angels and shepherds, which helped us to realize ourselves as candles of Joy or Love. God is giving a great responsibility to pass His love and joy to others. We are reminded to make room in our hearts, in our lives and in the lives of others to allow the Holy Spirit to bring us His love, joy and awareness of our saviour. Let's see what we are seeing in the mirror today.

Magi in the Mirror

"Then, opening their treasure-chests, they offered him gifts of gold, frankincense, and myrrh. And having been warned in a dream not to return to Herod, they left for their own country by another road." (Matthew 2:12).

If we see Magi in the mirror, that represents we became *Candles of Peace.* During Christmas time most of us lose peace because of many reasons. Many of us wish to have a peaceful Christmas, but we fail. But did we try to do something for making that peace around us? Wise men first read the sign of God. Did we ever try to read the notifications given by God? We know how to interpret the weather signs in the sky but we close our senses toward God and His signs. Secondly, they acted on the sign of God to find peace. They travelled thousand plus miles to find the Prince of Peace by following the star. To create a peaceful atmosphere around us, we don't even need to walk a thousand miles rather we just need to make a call or need to step into our next-door neighbour's house. Finally, they took another road, they realized the path which they came was not the path of peace and they changed their route. We are already melted, mashed and moulded by our Lord. Being lighted at Bethlehem, our Lord is asking us to make peace around us by reading and following His sign by choosing a different path in our life.

Making peace – do what we can

One day a terrible fire broke out in a forest – huge woodlands were suddenly engulfed by a raging wildfire. Being frightened, all the animals fled their homes and ran out of the forest. As they came to the edge of a stream, they stopped to watch the fire and they were feeling very discouraged and powerless. But a bird decided to do something. It swooped into the stream, picked up a few drops of water, went into the forest and put them on the fire. All the other animals watched in disbelief; some tried to discourage the hummingbird with comments like, "Don't bother, it is too much, you are too little, your wings will burn, your beak is too tiny, it's only a drop, you can't put out this fire." Then one of the animals shouted out and challenged the hummingbird in a mocking voice, "What do you think you are doing?" And the bird, without wasting time or losing a beat, looked back, and said, "I am doing what I can." After hearing that the elephants joined with the bird, then the monkeys, then gradually all the animals. That resulted in stopping the fire.

Looking at the world we may feel that, as a single candle what I can do to make peace. But believe in the God who transformed us. He took us not for surrendering ourselves into the world, but for making peace and victory for the glory of our

God. This Christmas, like the bird, just try what we can, that can bring peace around us. Don't forget there is a God, who is within us. When we are lighted at Bethlehem, His light will guide us, just follow the star.

Oh Lord, thank you for this new life.
You changed me to a candle of peace.
I was seeking through deserts and seas
Rivers and mounts, woods and leas
I waited for Your peace in tears and pains
Standing in the sun and rains
You gave the peace to quench my thirst
This peace is my precious treasure
Wealth of my life beyond all measure
Help me follow the star and make peace, till I take my last breath.

Day 24
Mirror time . . . moulded candles . . . moulded hearts

Today we are seeing the candle of hope in the mirror, the candle which reverts and sustains the love, joy, and peace.

Seeing a woman in the mirror

"There was also a prophetess, Anna, the daughter of Phanuel, of the tribe of Asher. She was very old; she had lived with her husband seven years after her marriage and then was a widow until she was eighty-four. She never left the temple but worshiped night and day, fasting and praying. Coming up to them at that very moment, she gave thanks to God and spoke about the child to all who were looking forward to the redemption of Jerusalem" (Luke 2:36-38).

Anna, a prophetess not part of the nativity story is appearing in the mirror today but truly represents the real meaning of Advent. Anna lived only seven years with her husband. Losing her husband after a few years of marriage must have been devastating, but her faith remained strong. After suffering through that tremendous loss, she devoted her life only to God. She did not let the loss of her husband change her faith or her love for the Lord. She was fasting and praying for the Lord. She was anxiously waiting for the Lord. Many might have asked her why she was not leaving the temple. She might have said the answer "I am waiting for the Lord". Can you imagine an 84-year-old lady talking about Messiah at the temple and waiting for him? If it happened now, we might say she is not normal. God was Anna's priority. She didn't just "know" He was first in her life, she "showed" it by her actions. *Romans 12:11 Never be lacking in zeal, but keep your spiritual fervour, serving the Lord.* Anna showed her hope to everyone around her. The mirror showed us Anna today, do you feel, are you reflecting Anna's hope in this Christmas? Our God made us with this level of hope. We need to keep that hope not only for Christmas but also for His Second Advent. If we believe Anna's image is our reflection, we are the ***Candle of Hope.***

Hope drives us in this Christmas

Four candles were burning slowly in the dark room. It was so quiet that you can hear their talk. The first candle said: "I am Peace, but nobody wants to support me. I suppose that I will die down." The flame of that candle began to slow down, and very soon it died. The second one told others, "I am Joy, people are not interested in me anymore, so I do not have any sense to burn." The flame of the candle disappeared instantly in a wind. The third candle began her speech very dreary: "I am Love; I do not have any forces to be on fire. Human beings reject me, and they do not want to realize the importance of my existence. They even forget to love their nearest and dearest." It also vanished with speed. Suddenly a little boy came into the room. He began to cry when he saw that three candles had already disappeared. "Why have you died? You should be in fire completely!" The fourth candle said "Stop crying! While I am still burning, we can help others because I am Hope!" The happy child took the candle of hope and lit other candles. The light of hope should never die in our lives. Joy, peace and love will always accompany hope.

Let's proclaim to the world. God changed me from frozen wax to an amazing fragrance-filled candle of Hope. Let's step together to Bethlehem with the candles of peace, joy and love. In the advent wreath, place all of us in the right place ready to be lighted.

Oh Lord, you are an awesome God.
You melted me, mashed me, and moulded me
When I was in the darkness, you held my hands.
Hope keeps me going, that longs for a better day
Hope keeps me rowing; Will helps me to reach far
Hope helps me rise each morning, which fills grace in my life
Hope tucks me in each night, that helps me to pray for
your will.
Oh Lord, help me to fill your hope in others.
Let me hope for your coming. . . and pass your joy, love
and peace.

Day 25
Lighted to Lighten by the Light of the Life

Miles passed, minds transformed, now at the manger as meaningful candles waiting to be lightened by the mighty light of the Life.

Light of the Life

"I am the light of the world" (John 8:12).

This beautiful Christmas morning, we are at Bethlehem in front of the Christ the Candle, *the light of the world, the light of all the life*. See in the manger, brighter than stars, the light is clear and dazzling *"a light to lighten the entire world"*. Just not for a specific group, but He is destined to shed His beams over the whole earth. As a preacher, He was luminous. Light penetrated the precept through and through as He made the very essence of purity apparent. His light cleared the law of the mists and fogs that the rabbinical writers had gathered around it. He shed light to the mindsets. His parables threw wondrous light upon the dispensation of the kingdom of heaven. He told about God the Father, willing to receive His prodigal children back again into His garden. His counsels and his cautions brought the final destinies of the righteous and the wicked into full view. His own life exhibited the power of love, the value of sympathy, and the virtue of forgiving injuries. His death gave yet more palpable evidence of unfaltering submission to the will of God, and unflinching self-sacrifice for the welfare of men. The sin and the sorrow, the shame, and the sentence, all vanish when His light fills our life. He is the lighthouse that throws its beams across the dark waters of human guilt and misery, warns humans, and guides them to Eden. A Saviour! God in human flesh! Our light, which we were waiting for days. Let us bow down and light ourselves with His light.

Lighted to Lighten

"You are the light of the world . . . let your light shine"
(Mathew. 4:14,16).

Jesus proclaimed. Every true Christian is called not only to speak of the wondrous saving work of Jesus Christ but also to manifest the fruit of that salvation in his own life. You are enlightened. God's light shines in and through us to bring healing to the world. Can we claim this promise? Can we live this affirmation in our daily life? This is God's vision and intent for our life – to be light and to reflect the light. Jesus said, *"Let your light so shine, so that all people will see your good works, your works of love, and give glory to God who is in heaven."* He lighted us; we need to shine His light to the lost people of the world and give them knowledge and lead them to God, Jesus, and salvation. Our Christianity is to be visible, to be seen and is to be noticed through our actions of love. People are to know we are Christian by what we say and by what we do. There is no such thing as a secret Christian. Our faith needs to shine no matter where we are, at work, at play, or at school. Our language must be filled with words about God. This light is not like a light with on/off switch. This is something we need to carry and need to pass to others till our last breath.

Mother who lighted the world with love

*A woman lay dying on a Calcutta pavement. Her feet were half eaten away by rats and ants. She had been lying there for days and no one had taken any notice of her. Then a nun came along. She was a tiny woman, dressed in a white sari which hung loosely about her and covered her head. She walked quickly, for she was always in a hurry. Her name was Mother Teresa. When she saw the woman on the pavement she stopped. She picked her up and carried her to a nearby hospital for treatment. She carried the light of God's love and passed it to everyone around her. Mother Teresa is an icon of kindness, love in action, compassion, sacrifice, service, frugality, a transformer of hearts and minds and a moral example that transcends culture, class and religion. Once she said, "Never worry about numbers. Help one person at a time and always start with the person nearest you." On 10 September 1946, Teresa experienced "the call within the call", or we can say she was **lighted to lighten by the light of the life**.*

As Mother said, never worry about the numbers, we saw the light, He lighted us. Now we need to carry the light, lighted at Bethlehem to lighten the people nearest to us, so that together we can fill the world with the light of life. Our journey is not ending at Bethlehem. Each of us has a purpose for being on this planet, when we know that purpose, we have the opportunity to manifest it. We should pass His Love, Joy, Peace, and Hope to others. Oh Lord, thank You for Your great Mercy on us, help us to carry Your light and light others. Amen.

My heart was frozen, with full of hatred
I closed my mind,

I didn't risk my time, for someone else's warmth.
My tears ceased due to frost, not another ever dropped.
I stayed in the freezing cold with lost hope and love.
Fear of pain and rejection, keeps the heart locked away . . .
I stayed away so no one could hurt me. I was away from
the Lord.

On an Advent Day, I heard a warm voice,
an angel's voice, about Emmanuel.

I wished, I really wished to see him.
I started my journey, it was hard . . .
I saw Mary melted her fears, and then Joseph cleared
his doubts.
I started melting . . .

A priest prayed with unbelief; a king became hungry
Scribes were confused, Jerusalem was afraid
The innkeeper was with frozen heart.
Their actions were reflections of my past.
I felt shame on myself.

But my Lord was near; He melted and purified me with a smile.
I was in a hurry to see the baby boy.

My Lord stopped me and mashed me
He mashed me with the fruits.
Fruits He named, love, joy, peace, forbearance,
Goodness, kindness, faithfulness, gentleness and self control

It was hurting me . . . I thought of running away.
But my heart was longing to see the baby.
After melting and mashing . . . Angels put me into the mould . . .
The Lord became my wick. I became God-centred.
I was waiting . . . Waiting with Simeon, a life spent waiting
I was about to ask question like John the Baptist.
But I learned to wait patiently

Days passed, I was taken out of the mould, and I rushed to
the mirror.
I saw many candles there; everyone was looking at the mirror
Some saw angels, some shepherds, some wise men, some Anna
They represented Joy, love, peace and hope.
I realised this waiting was a transformation of many minds
I started crying. I remembered, I was a frozen wax,
But He picked me, melted me, mashed me, and moulded me.
Now I am a candle with a meaning and purpose
He whispered," I am with you."
I remembered the angel's voice . . . Emmanuel . . ..

I stepped into Bethlehem.
The heaven opened, angels around
With wise men and Shepherds, I saw that bright light . . .
*He said, **"I am the light of the world."***

He came near and near, and lighted me . . ..
I filled the manger with fragrance of Holy Spirit . . .

He said *"**You are the light of the world; let your light shine. . ..**"*

I passed the light to others; Bethlehem was filled with candle lights . . .

I came to see the light, now I was lighted to lighten the world . . .

Oh, Lord . . .I love you; I love you for making me and lighting me.

My Journey with a God in my centre and light in my heart starts here.

*Candles greeted each other, **Merry Christmas . . .***

Emmanuel . . . Emmanuel . . . Emmanuel . . ..